A+
books

DINOSAUR FACT DIG

STEGOSAURUS
AND OTHER PLATED DINOSAURS
THE NEED-TO-KNOW FACTS

BY
KATHRYN CLAY

Consultant: Mathew J. Wedel, PhD
Associate Professor
Western University of Health Services

raintree

Raintree is an imprint of Capstone Global Library Limited, a company incorporated in England and Wales having its registered office at 264 Banbury Road, Oxford, OX2 7DY – Registered company number: 6695582

www.raintree.co.uk
myorders@raintree.co.uk
Text © Capstone Global Library Limited 2016
The moral rights of the proprietor have been asserted.

Edited by Michelle Hasselius
Designed by Kristi Carlson
Picture research by Wanda Winch
Production by Gene Bentdahl

ISBN 978 1 474 71939 1 (hardcover)
20 19 18 17 16
10 9 8 7 6 5 4 3 2 1

ISBN 978 1 474 71952 0 (paperback)
21 20 19 18 17
10 9 8 7 6 5 4 3 2 1

British Library Cataloguing in Publication Data
A full catalogue record for this book is available from the British Library.

ACKNOWLEDGEMENTS
All images by Jon Hughes except: MapArt (maps), Shuttershock: Elena Elisseeva, green gingko leaf, Jiang Hongyan, yellow gingko leaf, Taigi, paper background

Every effort has been made to contact copyrightholders of material reproduced in this book. Any omissions will be rectified in subsequent printings if notice is given to the publisher.

All the internet addresses (URLs) given in this book were valid at the time of going to press. However, due to the dynamic nature of the internet, some addresses may have changed, or sites may have changed or ceased to exist since publication. While the author and publisher regret any inconvenience this may cause readers, no responsibility for any such changes can be accepted by either the author or the publisher.

Printed and bound in China.

CONTENTS

STEGOSAURUS AND OTHER PLATED DINOSAURS

were slow-moving plant-eaters. They couldn't outrun hungry predators. But many of these dinosaurs had tall, pointy plates that made them dangerous.

Plated dinosaurs lived between 155 and 65 million years ago. While all of these dinosaurs had plates, no two dinosaurs looked the same. Hesperosaurus had short, wide plates. Chungkingosaurus' plates were long and looked like thin spikes. Find out about these plated plant-eaters and many more.

CHUNGKINGOSAURUS

PRONOUNCED: chung-KING-ah-SAWR-us

NAME MEANING: Chongqing lizard, fossils were found near Chongqing, China

TIME PERIOD LIVED: Late Jurassic Period, about 160 million years ago

LENGTH: 4 metres (13 feet)

WEIGHT: 227 kilograms (500 pounds)

TYPE OF EATER: herbivore

PHYSICAL FEATURES: thick, narrow plates on its back that looked like spikes

CHUNGKINGOSAURUS laid 20 to 30 eggs at a time.

Chungkingosaurus lived in the forests of what is now China.

N
W E
S

where this dinosaur lived

Parts of four **CHUNGKINGOSAURUS** skeletons have been found.

CHUNGKINGOSAURUS was one of the smallest stegosaurs. Stegosaurus was more than 10 times larger.

GIGANTSPINOSAURUS

PRONOUNCED: JIH-gant-SPIN-o-SAWR-us

NAME MEANING: giant-spined lizard

TIME PERIOD LIVED: Late Jurassic Period, more than 160 million years ago

LENGTH: 4.3 metres (14 feet)

WEIGHT: 680 kilograms (1,500 pounds)

TYPE OF EATER: herbivore

PHYSICAL FEATURES: sharp spikes on its shoulders, plates along its back

GIGANTSPINOSAURUS was one of the earliest stegosaurs.

Although **GIGANTSPINOSAURUS** had big shoulder spikes, the plates on its back were small.

Gigantspinosaurus lived in the forests of what is now central China.

where this dinosaur lived

N
W — E
S

The first **GIGANTSPINOSAURUS** fossils were discovered in 1985.

Fossilized skin from **GIGANTSPINOSAURUS** shows that the dinosaur was covered with scales.

GIGANTSPINOSAURUS got its name because of the two large spikes on its shoulders. The dinosaur had longer shoulder spikes than any other stegosaur.

GIGANTSPINOSAURUS used its spikes to protect itself against predators such as Yangchuanosaurus.

HESPEROSAURUS

PRONOUNCED: HES-per-ah-SAWR-us

NAME MEANING: western lizard

TIME PERIOD LIVED: Late Jurassic Period, about 150 million years ago

LENGTH: 6.4 metres (21 feet)

WEIGHT: 3.5 metric tons (3.9 tons)

TYPE OF EATER: herbivore

PHYSICAL FEATURES: short, wide plates on its back

HESPEROSAURUS had a set of four spikes on its tail. This is called a thagomizer.

HESPEROSAURUS' plates were covered in keratin. Human nails are also made of keratin.

Hesperosaurus lived in the prairies and forests of what is now Wyoming, USA.

N
W E
S

where this dinosaur lived

HESPEROSAURUS may have faced the Sun on cool days. The dinosaur's plates soaked up the Sun's heat to warm its body.

HUAYANGOSAURUS

PRONOUNCED: hwi-YANG-oh-SAWR-us

NAME MEANING: Huayang lizard, fossils were discovered near Huayang, China

TIME PERIOD LIVED: Middle Jurassic Period, about 165 million years ago

LENGTH: 4 metres (13 feet)

WEIGHT: 454 kilograms (1,000 pounds)

TYPE OF EATER: herbivore

PHYSICAL FEATURES: two rows of narrow plates on its back, sharp spikes on its shoulders and tail

Huayangosaurus lived in the forests of what is now China.

where this dinosaur lived

HUAYANGOSAURUS' plates are more narrow and pointed than most stegosaurs.

HUAYANGOSAURUS used its spiked tail to protect itself. One swing from its tail could hurt hungry predators.

13

HUAYANGOSAURUS was one of the first plated dinosaurs. It lived 20 million years before Stegosaurus.

HUAYANGOSAURUS had 14 teeth in the front of its mouth. The dinosaur used its front teeth to eat tough plants, such as ferns and conifers.

KENTROSAURUS

PRONOUNCED: KEN-tro-SAWR-us

NAME MEANING: pointed lizard

TIME PERIOD LIVED: Late Jurassic Period, about 150 million years ago

LENGTH: 4.5 metres (15 feet)

WEIGHT: 1 metric ton (1.1 tons)

TYPE OF EATER: herbivore

PHYSICAL FEATURES: two rows of pointed plates down its neck and back, sharp spikes on shoulders and tail

KENTROSAURUS' tail was longer than the rest of its body.

Kentrosaurus lived in swamps in what is now Tanzania.

N
W   E
S

where this dinosaur lived

KENTROSAURUS had a very good sense of smell.

Many **KENTROSAURUS** fossils were destroyed by bombs during Word War II (1939–1945).

LEXOVISAURUS

PRONOUNCED: lek-SOH-vi-SAWR-us

NAME MEANING: Lexovii lizard, after an ancient Celtic tribe in France

TIME PERIOD LIVED: Middle Jurassic Period, about 165 million years ago

LENGTH: 6 metres (20 feet)

WEIGHT: 2.4 metric tons (2.6 tons)

TYPE OF EATER: herbivore

PHYSICAL FEATURES: two rows of plates on its back, spikes along its tail

LEXOVISAURUS fossils are displayed at the National Museum of Natural History in Paris, France.

Lexovisaurus lived in what are now eastern England and France.

N
W   E
S

where this dinosaur lived

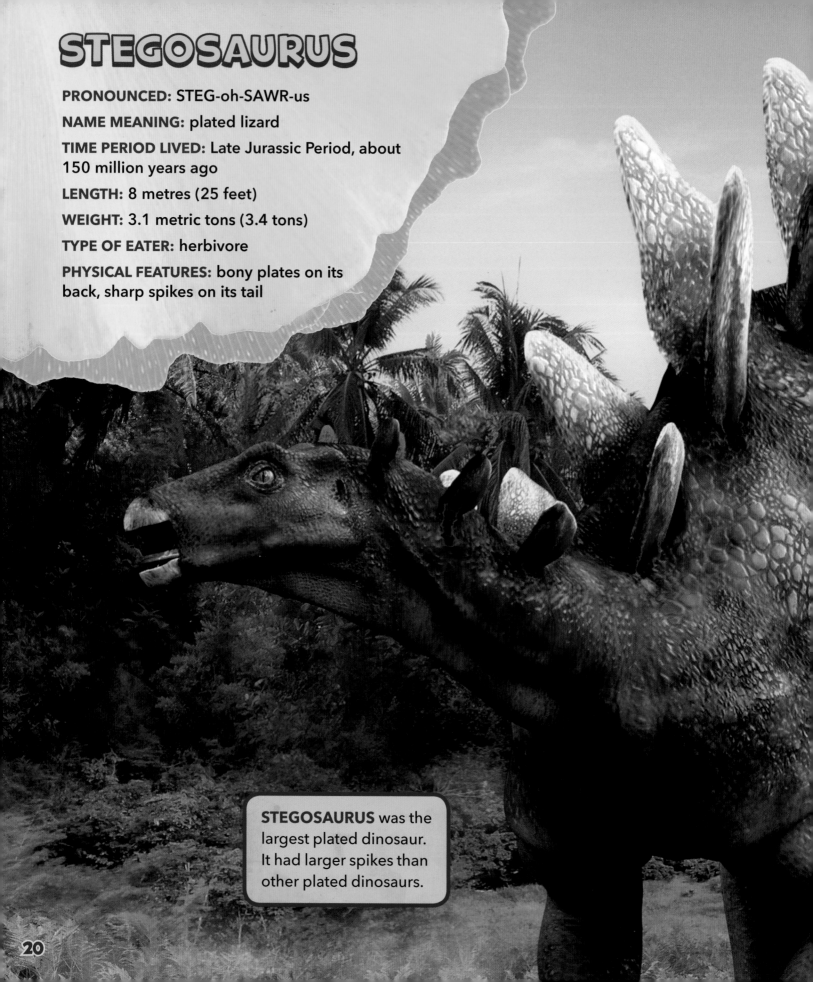

STEGOSAURUS

PRONOUNCED: STEG-oh-SAWR-us

NAME MEANING: plated lizard

TIME PERIOD LIVED: Late Jurassic Period, about 150 million years ago

LENGTH: 8 metres (25 feet)

WEIGHT: 3.1 metric tons (3.4 tons)

TYPE OF EATER: herbivore

PHYSICAL FEATURES: bony plates on its back, sharp spikes on its tail

STEGOSAURUS was the largest plated dinosaur. It had larger spikes than other plated dinosaurs.

Stegosaurus lived in the forests and swamps of North America.

N
W ◆ E
S

■ where this dinosaur lived

Fossils show **STEGOSAURUS** fought the predator Allosaurus. Some Allosaurus fossils have holes from Stegosaurus spikes. Some Stegosaurus plates have been found with Allosaurus bite marks.

STEGOSAURUS tore leaves off plants with its bony beak. It chewed the leaves with its back teeth.

The first **STEGOSAURUS** fossil was discovered in Colorado, USA in 1876.

STEGOSAURUS travelled in herds. This may have protected the dinosaur from predators.

STEGOSAURUS' plates were made out of keratin.

TUOJIANGOSAURUS

PRONOUNCED: TOO-oh-GEE-an-GO-SAWR-us

NAME MEANING: Tuo River lizard

TIME PERIOD LIVED: Late Jurassic Period, about 160 million years ago

LENGTH: 6.7 metres (22 feet)

WEIGHT: 2.8 metric tons (3.1 tons)

TYPE OF EATER: herbivore

PHYSICAL FEATURES: plates on its back, spikes on its tail

TUOJIANGOSAURUS looked similar to Stegosaurus. Both dinosaurs had flat, thick plates.

Tuojiangosaurus lived in the forests of what is now China.

N
W   E
S

where this
dinosaur lived

TUOJIANGOSAURUS was prey for the fearsome predator Yangchuanosaurus.

25

YINGSHANOSAURUS

PRONOUNCED: ying-SHAN-oh-SAWR-us

NAME MEANING: Golden Hills reptile, fossils were discovered in Yingshan, China

TIME PERIOD LIVED: Late Jurassic Period, about 155 million years ago

LENGTH: 4 to 5 metres (13 to 16 feet)

WEIGHT: 1.5 metric tons (1.6 tons)

TYPE OF EATER: herbivore

PHYSICAL FEATURES: long shoulder spikes that looked like wings

Paleontologists do not know a lot about this dinosaur. Only one **YINGSHANOSAURUS** skeleton has been discovered. But it is missing.

Yingshanosaurus lived in the forests of what is now China.

where this dinosaur lived

YINGSHANOSAURUS may have travelled in herds.

YINGSHANOSAURUS has a similar name to another dinosaur called Yangchuanosaurus. But the two dinosaurs were very different. Yangchuanosaurus was a meat-eater that walked on two legs.

GLOSSARY

BEAK hard, pointed part of an animal's mouth

CONIFER tree with cones and narrow leaves called needles

FERN plant with feathery leaves and no flowers; ferns usually grow in damp places

FOSSIL remains of an animal or plant from millions of years ago that have turned to rock

HERBIVORE animal that eats only plants

HERD group of the same kind of animals that live and travel together

JURASSIC PERIOD second period of the Mesozoic Era; the Jurassic Period was from 200 to 145 million years ago

KERATIN hard substance that forms a person's fingernails and toenails

PALEONTOLOGIST scientist who studies fossils

PLATE flat, bony growth

PRAIRIE large area of flat grassland

PREDATOR animal that hunts other animals for food

PRONOUNCE say a word in a certain way

SPIKE sharp, pointy object; some dinosaurs used spikes to defend themselves

SWAMP area of wet, spongy ground

THAGOMIZER tail of a stegosaur dinosaur that has four to 10 spikes

WORLD WAR II war in which the United States, France, Great Britain, the Soviet Union and other countries defeated Germany, Italy and Japan; World War II lasted from 1939 to 1945

COMPREHENSION QUESTIONS

1. How did Gigantspinosaurus get its name? Use the text to help you with your answer.

2. Dinosaurs such as Hesperosaurus have thagomizers at the ends of their tails. What is a thagomizer?

3. Yingshanosaurus and Yangchuanosaurus have similar names. How are these dinosaurs different?

READ MORE

Dinosaurs (First Facts), Charlie Gardner (DK Publishing, 2012)

Dinosaurs in our Street, David West (Franklin Watts, 2015)

A Weekend with Dinosaurs (Fantasy Field Trips), Claire Throp (Raintree, 2014)

WEBSITES

www.nhm.ac.uk/discover/dino-directory/index.html

At this Natural History Museum website you can learn more about dinosaurs through sorting them by name, country and even body shape!

www.show.me.uk/section/dinosaurs

This website has loads of fun things to do and see, including a dinosaur mask you can download and print, videos, games, and Top Ten lists.

INDEX